First published in the United States in 2003 by Chronicle Books LLC.

Copyright © 2002 by Albin Michel Jeunesse.
Translation © 2003 by Chronicle Books LLC.
Originally published in France in 2002 by Albin Michel Jeunesse
under the title *Les contraires de Didou*.

English type design by Jessica Dacher.
Typeset in Jennerik and ITC Bailey Sans.
Manufactured in Malaysia.

Library of Congress Cataloging-in-Publication Data
Got, Yves.
[Contraires de Didou. English]
Sam's opposites / by Yves Got.
p. cm.
"Originally published in France by Albin Michel Jeunesse
under the title *Les contraires de Didou*."
Summary: Sam the bunny rabbit introduces such pairs of opposites
as dirty/clean, top/bottom, whole/broken and angry/calm.
ISBN 0-8118-4077-8
1. English language — Synonyms and antonyms-Juvenile literature.
[1. English language — Synonyms and antonyms.] I. Title.
PE1591.G64 2003
428.1 — dc21
2002152666

Distributed in Canada by Raincoast Books
9050 Shaughnessy Street, Vancouver, British Columbia V6P 6E5

10 9 8 7 6 5 4 3 2 1

Chronicle Books LLC
85 Second Street, San Francisco, California 94105

www.chroniclekids.com

Sam's Opposites

by Yves Got

chronicle books · san francisco

Front

Back

Noisy

Quiet

Full

Empty

Fast

Slow

Sad

Happy

Dirty

Clean

Top

Bottom

Closed

Open

Brave

Scared

Hard

Soft

Sick

Well

Small

Big

Friends

Enemies

Whole

Broken

In front

In back

Hello

Good-bye

Wet

Dry

Serious

Silly

Messy

Neat

Angry

Calm

In

Out

Above

Below

Standing

Sitting

Cold

Warm

Careful

Clumsy

Heavy

Light

Friendly

Unfriendly

Black

White